LOOK!
IT'S JESUS!

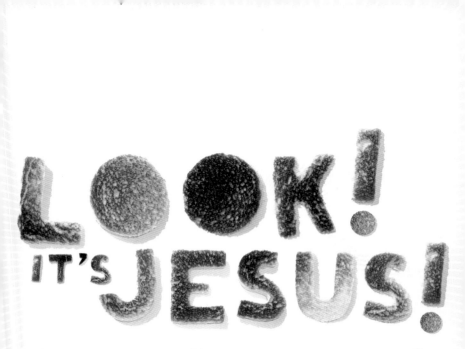

LOOK! IT'S JESUS!

❧ Amazing 𝕳𝖔𝖑𝖞 𝕍𝖎𝖘𝖎𝖔𝖓𝖘 In Everyday Life ❧

HARRY AND SANDRA CHORON

CHRONICLE BOOKS

SAN FRANCISCO

All photographs used with permission. All photographs courtesy of the contributors listed, with the following exceptions: "The Nun Bun" (photo by Mark Tucker); "Buddha Beehive" (photo by Elizabeth Nida, the *Rochester Post-Bulletin*); "Paper Towel Jesus" (photo by Peter Solomon); and "Bone Jesus" (courtesy of Gife.2ya.com). "Shower Jesus," "Frying Pan Jesus," "Grilled Cheese Virgin Mary," "Pierogi Jesus," "The Pope's Mitre Nacho Chip," "Pretzel Mary," "Tree Trunk Mary," and "Firewood Mary" courtesy of the Golden Palace Casino (GoldenPalace.com).

Library of Congress Cataloging-in-Publication Data

Choron, Harry.
  Look! it's Jesus! : amazing holy visions in everyday life / Harry and Sandra Choron.
      p. cm.
  ISBN 978-0-8118-7000-9 (pbk.)
 1. Parapsychology—Religious aspects. 2. Signs and symbols. 3. Experience (Religion) 4. Icons—Miscellanea. I. Choron, Sandra. II. Title.

  BL65.P3C46 2009
  204'.2—dc22

2009032759

Manufactured in China

Jacket design by Michael Morris
Interior design by Harry Choron, March Tenth Inc.

10 9 8 7 6 5 4 3 2

Chronicle Books LLC
680 Second Street
San Francisco, CA 94107
www.chroniclebooks.com

The authors would like to dedicate this book to our contributors, whose generosity of spirit served as a constant source of inspiration during the creation of this book. We would also like to thank Steve Mockus, Emilie Sandoz, Becca Cohen, Erin Thacker, and Michael Morris at Chronicle Books for their faith in the project and for their hard work and creativity.

> # "The whole world is charged with the glory of God."
>
> —THOMAS MERTON

Writer and philosopher Thomas Merton (1915–1968) saw God manifest everywhere. He is not alone. For thousands of years, religious visions have appeared in both unusual and everyday circumstances: Moses found God in a burning bush, Joan of Arc spoke to Him in a field in France, and Francis of Assisi was visited by Him in the rural hills of Italy. In 1858, 14-year-old Bernadette Soubirous saw the Virgin Mary in the woods near her hometown of Lourdes, and the small French village has since attracted many millions of pilgrims—averaging 5 million per year.

It's in this context of divine revelation that we can best understand Maria Rubio's discovery of the image of Jesus in a freshly-made tortilla. In 1977, Rubio was preparing her husband's breakfast of homemade burritos when she flipped over a tortilla and saw Jesus's face burned into its surface by the heat of the skillet. Word of the discovery travelled fast, and by that afternoon a line of the faithful and the curious stretched out the door of Rubio's home in the small town of Lake Arthur, New Mexico. In the years since Rubio's discovery, tens of thousands of people have made the pilgrimage to see the tortilla.

These days, discoveries like Rubio's are quickly picked up and popularized by the mass media. In June of 2003, an image of the Virgin Mary appeared in a window at Milton Hospital, near Boston, Massachusetts, caused by chemicals leaking onto an enclosed pane of glass. The weekend of its discovery, the BBC reported that more than 25,000 pilgrims visited the building to marvel at the image. In April of 2005, locals in Chicago, Illinois, noticed a salt stain on the wall of a freeway underpass that resembled the Madonna. Hundreds of visitors made the trek to see the stain and passersby set up an impromptu shrine to the image, which drew international news coverage and even inspired a play.

Collected here are dozens of documented religious visions, along with detailed descriptions of the discoveries by the people who found them. These images—of Mother Teresa, Jesus, the Virgin Mary, the Buddha, and others— might once have been confined to the villages in which they appeared, known only in local lore. Today, we are fortunate to live in an era of advanced personal digital technology, when unique religious experiences like these can be shared with others around the world. These amazing images can appear anywhere—in trees, gemstones, sandwiches, snacks, woodgrain, and outer space. And now, thanks to this book, we can appreciate them together for the first time.

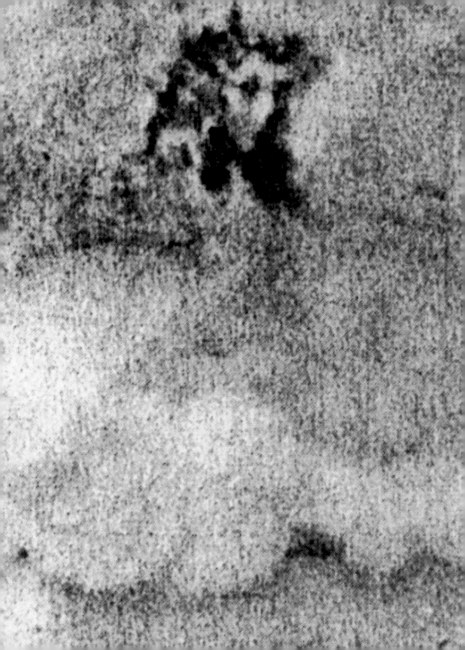

❧ TORTILLA JESUS ❧

On October 5, 1977, Maria Rubio was making fresh tortillas for her husband's breakfast when she came across a startling discovery: while cooking, the face of Jesus had been burned onto the surface of a tortilla by the heat of the skillet. Maria's husband, Eduardo, and their daughter, Rosy, recognized the image as well.

Even in the small town of Lake Arthur, New Mexico, word traveled fast. "That afternoon when I drove in from school, there was already a line of people waiting in front of my parents' house to go in and see the tortilla," says Rosy Rubio. "It was amazing."

The Rubio family built a shrine to the tortilla in their backyard, where it stayed for many years and was visited by many thousands of people. However, heat and time warped the image of Jesus on the tortilla's surface, and in 2006 it was dropped and broken during a show-and-tell at a local elementary school. Although the image of Christ is no longer very recognizable in the broken pieces, the Rubios still keep them in their home.

—CREATED BY MARIA RUBIO, LAKE ARTHUR, NEW MEXICO

⚜ AGATE VIRGIN MARY ⚜

Ricardo and Claudia Birnie found this gem, which contains an image of
the Virgin Mary, in the collection of an agate dealer in Buenos Aires.
"We found this beautiful agate about six years ago," the Birnies recall.
"It captured our interest and we just had to have it. We are now very
pleased to be able to share it with others."

—APPEARED TO RICARDO AND CLAUDIA BIRNIE,
BUENOS AIRES, ARGENTINA

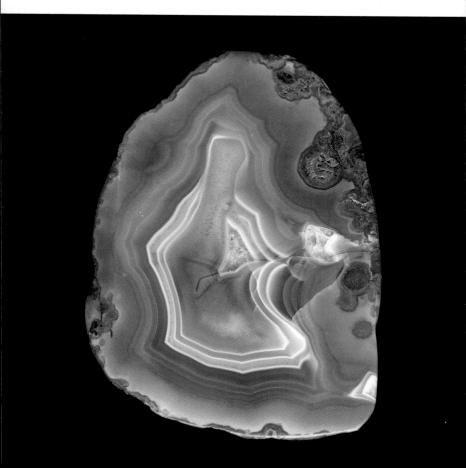

✧ ROCK MARY ✧

"This rock was found outside of Las Vegas about seven years ago, and it was first given to me upside down, looking like a smiley face," recalls Debbie Baumgartner. "But then I turned it around and saw the image. Everyone I show it to just goes bananas over it. Some of them even cry."

—DISCOVERED BY DEBBIE BAUMGARTNER, PALM BAY, FLORIDA

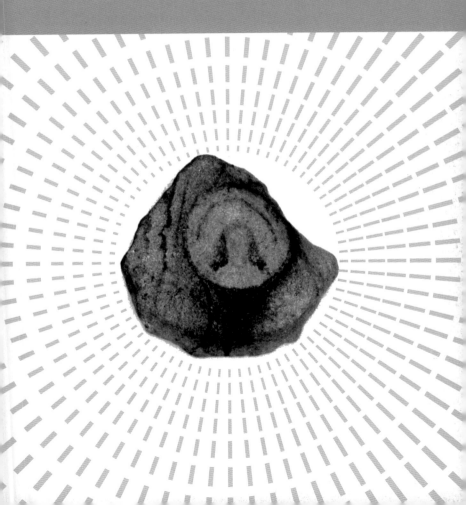

❧ BASEBALL JESUS ❧

In June of 2009, Michelle De Serf found a baseball on the ground near the back door to her kitchen. "The ball had a smudge with an image of Jesus on it," she recalls. "I picked it up and showed it to my husband, Craig, who was astonished. I then showed it to my kids and they saw the face of Jesus, as well. They thought it was the neatest thing they'd ever seen."

—FOUND BY MICHELLE DE SERF, SUGAR LAND, TEXAS

✣ THROWING ROCK JESUS ✣

Mackenzie Katzfey's family was camping near a small river in Southwestern Missouri, enjoying the usual outdoor activities. "About our second day there, my mom and I started throwing rocks in the water," Katzfey remembers. "But we always looked at them before we threw them in. I came across a rock and noticed right away that it looked like Jesus. As I showed it to my family, we remembered the Bible verse in Psalms 18:2, 'The Lord is my rock . . .' I thought it was cool and sort of funny."

—DISCOVERED BY MACKENZIE KATZFEY, SPRINGDALE, ARIZONA

❧ HANDBAG JESUS ❧

In July of 2009, Barbara Litwiller put one of her handbags up for auction on eBay. She took several photos of the bag for the listing, trying to catch it from all angles. After she uploaded the photos to her computer, she noticed that a face seemed to be staring back at her from the side of the bag. "It is a strange feeling to look at a photograph of a normal looking handbag and see an image that could be Jesus looking back at you," she says.

—REVEALED TO BARBARA LITWILLER, SARASOTA, FLORIDA

✤ TOWEL JESUS ✤

In February of 2009, Steven Smith decided to tie-dye some dish towels. "I wanted to liven up doing the dishes," he says. When he unfolded them the next day, he recalls, "I discovered the Jesus towel. People that see it say it's kind of creepy. You can see the cross, and kind of hovering behind it with his arms outstretched is a glowing Jesus."

—REVEALED TO STEVEN SMITH, BATAVIA, ILLINOIS

✿ TREE TRUNK MARY ✿

This image of the Virgin Mary, which can be seen on the bark of a tree in South Dallas, Texas, was first noticed in November of 2005. The discovery received widespread attention from American and Mexican media alike, and since the Virgin's appearance, thousands of visitors and believers have made the pilgrimage to see her. A shrine with candles, rosary beads, and bottles of holy water now adorns the foot of the tree.

—FOUND IN SOUTH DALLAS, TEXAS

❧ WOODBLOCK MARY ❧

Lela Dawkins, a printing room employee in Akron, Ohio, found this woodblock in the warehouse where she works. The block was just one of many shipped to the warehouse by the Williamsburg Paper Company, but when she picked it up, Dawkins saw an image of the Virgin Mary.

—SHARED BY LELA DAWKINS AND TIM REICHENBACH, AKRON, OHIO

❧ ASHTRAY JESUS ❧

Kurt Hamilton-Foster lives in a former Church of England church in NSW Australia. After hosting a party the week before Christmas, he was amazed to find this image of Jesus's face in an old ashtray used by his guests during the festivities. "We do not have any explanation for the weird, uncanny face that peers back at you from the ashes," Hamilton-Foster remarks. "Many smokers used that particular ashtray throughout the evening. It was clean and featureless when the party began. Obviously, the ashes alone could not explain the face. The features of Jesus have been literally burnt into the enamel surface."

—REVEALED TO KURT HAMILTON-FOSTER,
KEERRONG, AUSTRALIA

❧ THE NUN BUN ❧

This cinnamon bun bearing the image of Mother Teresa was first discovered at the Bongo Java Café in Belmont, Tennessee. The café had the bun on display for about ten years, until Christmas day in 2007, when the bun was stolen. Bob Bernstein, the owner of Bongo Java, offered a $5,000 reward for its recovery. When it eventually turned up in a thrift shop, Bernstein was delighted to find it intact.

—DISCOVERED BY BOB BERNSTEIN, BELMONT, TENNESSEE

❧ WASHBURN GUITAR JESUS ❧

In December of 2008, the bearded face of Jesus was discovered on a Washburn Dreadnought D46SP acoustic guitar at the Instrumental Music and Sound shop in Ludington, Michigan. The face is visible in the body's maple grain, just below the bridge. "I've been here for twenty-seven years and I've never seen anything close to that," says Jeff Hoyer, an employee at the store. "The face is so clear."

—APPEARED IN THE INSTRUMENTAL MUSIC AND SOUND SHOP,
LUDINGTON, MICHIGAN

⚜ THE POPE'S MITRE NACHO CHIP ⚜

The Chadwick family was eating a bag of Doritos in March of
2005 when they came upon a chip in the exact shape of the Pope's
hat, which is known as a mitre. Shortly after its discovery, the
Chadwicks decided that it would be unfair to keep the tortilla chip
from the rest of the world and sold it to the Golden Palace Casino.

—DISCOVERED BY THE CHADWICK FAMILY,
SALEM, MASSACHUSETTS

❧ OYSTER SHELL JESUS ❧

In 2006, Frank and Pauline Titone took a summer boat trip to the Tomoka River Basin in Ormond, Florida. Admiring shells on the beach, they discovered a likeness of Christ in one discarded oyster. "This finding is more precious to us than a pearl in an oyster shell would have been," they say.

—DISCOVERED BY FRANK AND PAULINE TITONE,
ORMOND, FLORIDA

❧ BUTTERNUT WOOD JESUS ❧

In 2007, Cindy Hurt's husband Robert was working at a small cabinet factory in Mentone, Indiana, when he came across this piece of butternut wood. He made the discovery while cutting through a stack of lumber. "I don't even have to explain what he saw," says Cindy Hurt, pointing out the image of Jesus on the wood's surface. "He knew it was something that other people would find interesting, and started showing it to everybody. People were so amazed!"

—DISCOVERED BY ROBERT AND CINDY HURT, MENTONE, INDIANA

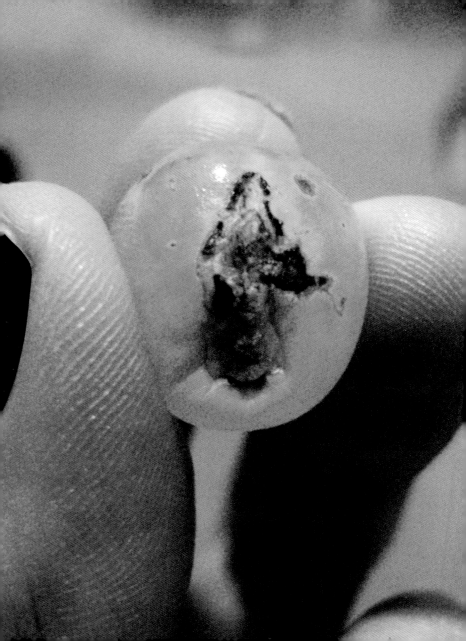

❈ ROTTING GRAPE ❈ VIRGIN MARY

Makeup artist Becky Ginn was about to throw out a bunch of rotting grapes when she noticed a familiar image on one of them. "I turned it over, and said, 'Oh, that looks like the Virgin Mary.' It was the first thing that popped into my head." The grape is now stored in her freezer.

—REVEALED TO BECKY GINN, ARLINGTON, TEXAS

❦ FIREWOOD MARY ❦

The owner of this block of wood, known only by her first name, Faith, was seconds away from throwing it into her stove when the image of the Virgin Mary appeared to her. Having never considered herself a religious person, she was amazed to see the Virgin, complete with halo, on the block of wood, and could not bring herself to burn it.

—APPEARED IN JANESVILLE, WISCONSIN

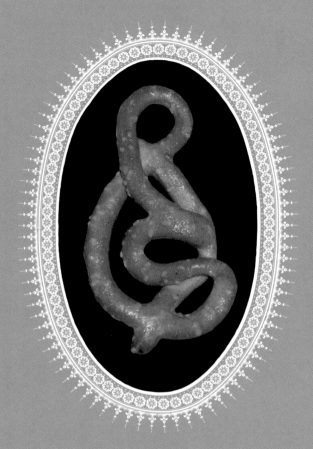

✤ PRETZEL MADONNA AND CHILD ✤

Twelve-year-old Crysta Naylor was snacking and watching television with her family when she discovered this pretzel, shaped like the Virgin Mary holding baby Jesus. "We only paid $3.29 for the whole bag," says her mother, Machelle.

—APPEARED TO CRYSTA NAYLOR, ST. PAUL, MINNESOTA

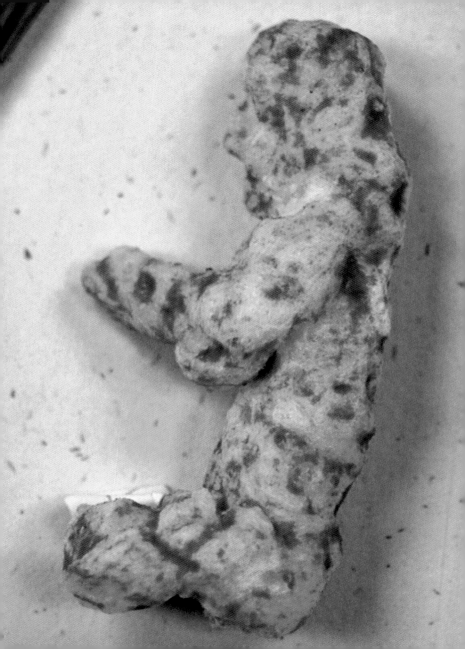

✤ CHEESUS ✤

In 2004, Steve Cragg, youth director at Memorial
Drive United Methodist Church in Houston, Texas,
came across this odd-shaped Cheeto while snacking.
"I do not think that God makes Cheetos that look
like Jesus," Cragg explains, "but I do know that God
reveals himself to us in amazing ways. This Cheeto
has generated a lot of positive discussion within our
youth group about how we can see God in the world
today." Cragg named his discovery "Cheesus."

—DISCOVERED BY STEVE CRAGG, HOUSTON, TEXAS

❧ WATERMARK MARY ❧

In 1994, locals in Clearwater, Florida, noticed that a large watermark had formed on the outer glass of a downtown bank. Unbelievably, the stain seemed to have taken the form of the Virgin Mary. For years, the watermark drew hundreds of pilgrims and tourists to the small town. Sadly, several years ago, a vandal threw a rock through the glass, shattering the Virgin's head. Despite the damage, the water mark continues to astonish; at night the face of Jesus appears on the window

—SHARED BY TILLMAN HAUSHERR,
BERLIN, GERMANY

❧ NIGHTTIME WATERMARK JESUS ❧

The watermark Mary that appeared in the outer glass of a bank
in Clearwater, Florida (see previous page) reveals another holy
figure at night, when the face of a tear-shedding Jesus appears
on the belly of the Virgin Mary.

—SHARED BY SIMONE DE SANTI, MIAMI, FLORIDA

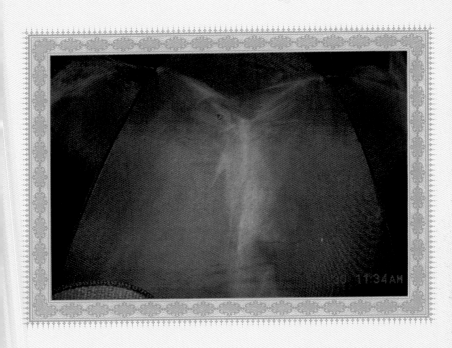

❧ UMBRELLA JESUS ❧

In the summer of 2007, Chris Brelo and his wife were just finishing up dinner with his parents when it started raining. Having arrived without an umbrella, they had to borrow one from the back of his parents' closet. "To our surprise, the first thing we saw when we opened the umbrella was an image of Jesus Christ on the Cross," says Brelo. "We all just stood there in silence staring at the image. We could clearly see Jesus. We saw his legs crossed, his arms spread, and his head bowed, and we could even see his hair and beard."

—APPEARED TO CHRISTOPHER J. BRELO, AKRON, OHIO

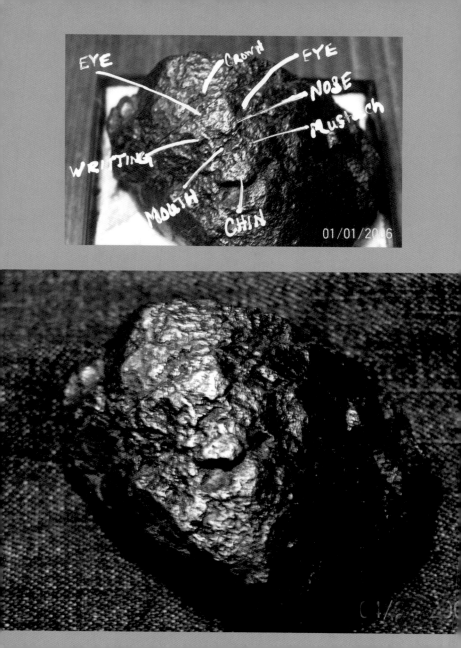

✤ METEORITE JESUS ✤

A meteor landed in Terrence Cotton's backyard just before Christmas in 2007. The extremely rare rock has been valued at $10,000–$15,000, but to Mr. Cotton, who sees the image of Jesus on its surface, the object is priceless. "To me, it's a miracle, period," he says. "I think it's a really big deal that Jesus Christ is on this rock. It's just unreal."

—FOUND BY TERRENCE COTTON, ABILENE, TEXAS

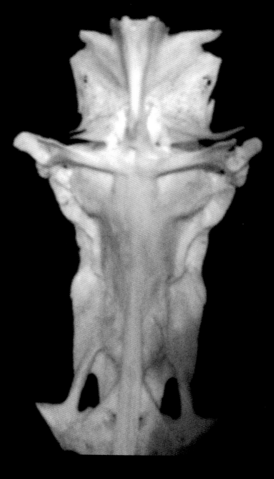

✤ BONE JESUS ✤

Bill Tomsick discovered this remarkable fishbone during a casual stroll on a Florida beach. "I did some research and found out that the fish was a Gaff Top Sail Catfish—no other fish has this kind of bone," says Tomsick. Local lore has it that catching one of these fish is considered a stroke of luck that will bring the fisherman good fortune.

—FOUND BY BILL TOMSICK, CAPE CORAL, FLORIDA

❧ CAVE ROCK JESUS ❧

In May of 2009, Shari Martino and her mother, Maria Goldman, decided to explore a cave near Sullivan, Missouri. Flashlight in hand, Martino was hoping to find some fossils or arrowheads to collect. At the mouth of the cave, however, she noticed a peculiar-looking rock on the ground. Martino recalls calling to her mother, "Mom, check this out! It's a Jesus rock!" The image of Jesus remained clearly visible even after they brought the rock out of the cave and into the light of day.

—REVEALED TO SHARI MARTINO AND MARIA GOLDMAN,
CRYSTAL RIVER, FLORIDA

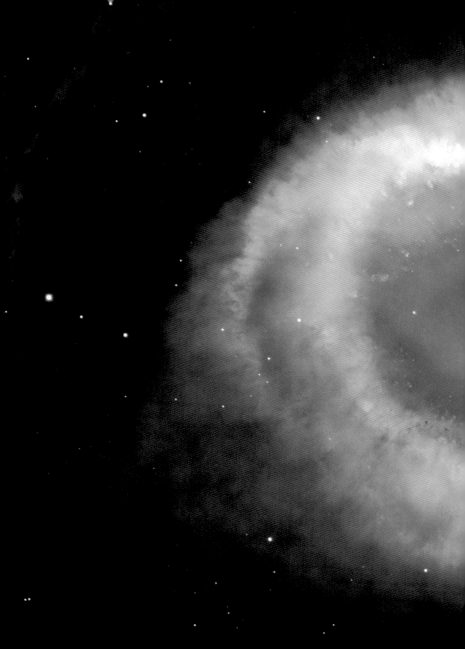

✿ THE HELIX NEBULA ✿

This photo of the Helix Nebula was taken by the Hubble Space Telescope in May of 2003. The formation pictured here, dubbed "The Eye of God" by the scientists who first laid eyes upon it, is "a trillion-mile-long tunnel of glowing gases."

—COURTESY OF NASA, HUBBLE TELESCOPE

❧ ICE JESUS ❧

Tom Bredesen took this photo along the banks of the Ontonagon River in Michigan's Upper Peninsula. "This ice sculpture, created by nature, amazed our friends and family alike," Bredesen says. "There is a light above Jesus that surrounds Him, and the countenance of His face appears to be one at peace."

—CAPTURED BY TOM BREDESEN, BOND FALLS, MICHIGAN

❈ PIEROGI JESUS ❈

Donna Lee discovered the face of Jesus while cooking
pierogis on Palm Sunday in 2005. "The last one
I flipped over was Jesus," she says. "I flipped the
spatula, and my husband goes, 'What? There's Jesus!'"

—PREPARED BY DONNA LEE, TOLEDO, OHIO

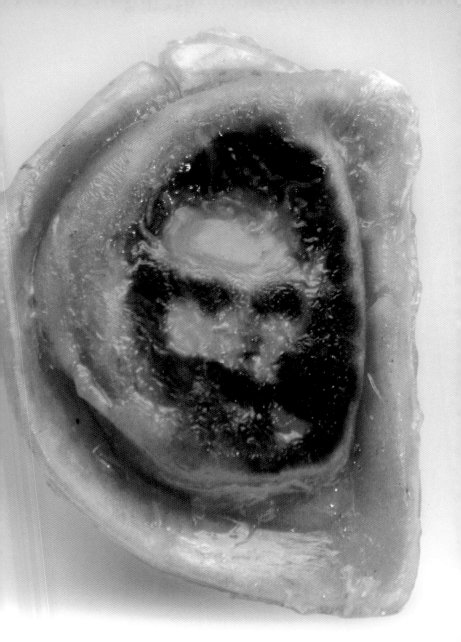

❧ SEASHELL VIRGIN MARY ❧
AND BABY

In August of 2008, while searching for shells on the coast of Myrtle Beach, South Carolina, Pam Smith found this unique seashell. "I immediately saw the image of the Virgin Mary holding a faceless baby," she recalls. "My husband and children were amazed. I stored it for almost a year, curious to see if the image would fade—it didn't. On this tiny shell is truly an amazing gift from God."

—SHARED BY TODD AND PAM SMITH, STAR, NORTH CAROLINA

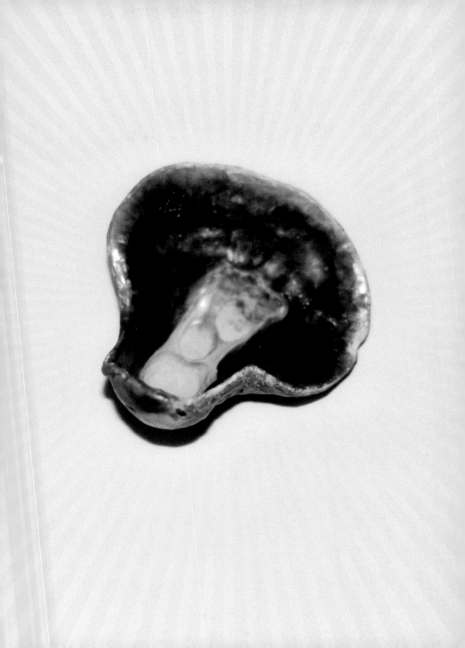

❧ WONDROUS CROSS JESUS ❧

Douglas Hamm first spotted this rock formation, which he calls "Wondrous Cross," while taking photographs in Arizona's Canyon de Chelly. "I feel very blessed that God gave me the opportunity to photograph that image," Hamm says. "It has probably been there for 1,000 years, but I was fortunate to be the one to find it." Hamm, a photographer who specializes in devotional art, describes the image as "Jesus on the cross with His head bowed, a crown of thorns on His head, the image of a lamb, a dove carrying a branch, and three crosses."

—REVEALED TO DOUGLAS HAMM, ROOSEVELT, ARIZONA

❧ ROCK JESUS ❧

Sonia Chamberlain found this rock while hiking near Lake Havasu City in 2008. She didn't notice anything unusual about it at first and threw it into her backpack along with the other rocks that she'd picked up on her hike. It wasn't until she had returned home and washed the stones that she recognized Jesus. "I was astonished because the detail of the hair and crown of thorns was perfect," she says. "For it to have formed in nature is amazing."

—REVEALED TO SONIA CHAMBERLAIN,
LAKE HAVASU CITY, ARIZONA

❈ CLOSET DOOR MARY ❈

Pepe Garcia found this door, featuring an image of the Virgin Mary, while out shopping at his local Home Depot. After he'd purchased it and taken it home, he casually asked a few friends if they saw anything—they all confirmed his vision. A local TV station featured the door on their evening news program, calling it a "divine image."

—SHARED BY CHRISTINE AND PEPE GARCIA, HOUSTON, TEXAS

✥ FRYING PAN JESUS ✥

After whipping up a lemon mustard cream sauce for dinner, an Australian cook accidentally placed the saucepan back on the hot stove. When he returned to the kitchen, he found that the remaining sauce was burnt onto the pan. The cook rinsed the pan and attempted to dislodge the charred bits of sauce with a spoon, but after a few moments of cleaning he noticed an image of Jesus staring back at him from the pan. He says that the burnt image of Christ restored his faith, and he hopes it can do the same for others.

—APPEARED TO AN ANONYMOUS COOK IN AUSTRALIA

❧ GRILLED CHEESE ❧ VIRGIN MARY

In 1994, Diane Duyser was getting ready to eat a grilled cheese sandwich when she saw the face of the Virgin Mary staring back at her on the toasted bread. "I went to take a bite out of it, and then I saw this lady looking back at me," she explains. Duyser wrapped the sandwich in a plastic bag and left it in her freezer for the next nine years. In 2003 she put the sandwich up for auction on eBay with the proviso that it was "not intended for consumption." The sandwich was eventually purchased by the Golden Palace Casino for $28,000.

—REVEALED TO DIANE DUYSER, HOLLYWOOD, FLORIDA

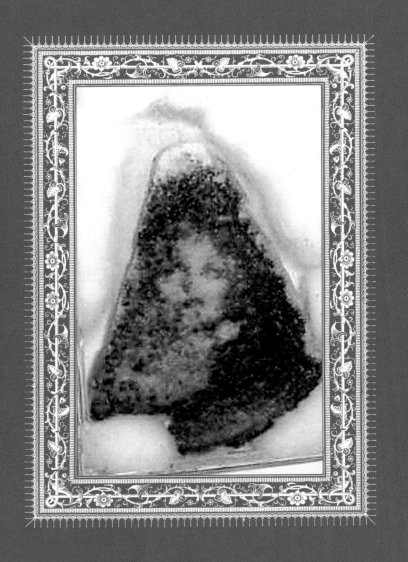

❧ CLOUD JESUS WITH ANGELS ❧

In December of 2008, Chris Kiely and his family were relaxing in the backyard of their farm in Australia when they saw a storm start to roll in. Kiely took dozens of photos of the storm, trying to capture its various stages. "There were remarkable cloud formations with captivating images, and a display of vibrant, brilliant colors, the likes of which we had never seen before," he remembers. When he developed the pictures, he noticed an image of Jesus surrounded by angels in one of the shots.

—APPEARED TO CHRIS KIELY, MOAMA, AUSTRALIA

❧ POTATO CHIP DEVIL ❧

James Charette found this potato chip while enjoying a bag of barbeque flavored snacks at a family gathering. Taking a pause between bites, he glanced down at the chip in his hand and received quite a shock—there amidst the seasoning was an image of a demonic face.

—DISCOVERED BY JAMES CHARETTE, FT. MYERS, FLORIDA

❧ SHOWER JESUS ❧

Jeffrey Rigo first caught sight of Christ's face in this water-stained piece of plaster while stepping out of the shower on June 11, 2005. Rigo cut the plaster from the wall and dubbed the divine stain "Shower Jesus."

—REVEALED TO JEFFREY RIGO, PITTSBURGH, PENNSYLVANIA

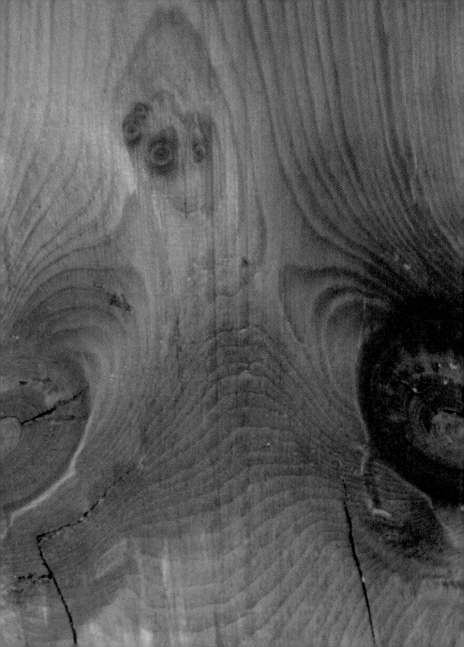

❧ WOODEN PLANK MOSES ❧

One afternoon in 2006, Steven Graves decided to remove some decaying lumber from an old farmhouse near his home in Peterborough, New Hampshire. As he moved the century-old logs, Graves noticed a distinct facial pattern on one particular piece of wood. "I showed my family the image, and after some initial rolled eyes, they thought it was sort of cool. Someone suggested that it looked like Moses with the Ten Commandments. If this image of mine brings a smile to someone's face or solidifies their faith, then that would be wonderful," he says.

—DISCOVERED BY STEVEN GRAVES,
PETERBOROUGH, NEW HAMPSHIRE

❈ MARBLE JESUS ❈

In June of 2008, the Verona Marble Company detected a special piece of material in their inventory. "Some say the slab resembles our Lord Jesus Christ," observes John M. Ganster, Jr., director of operations. "We don't profess that this slab is somehow divinely inspired, but we do enjoy the resemblance that it seems to have."

—SHARED BY JOHN M. GANSTER, JR., DALLAS, TEXAS

✤ BUNK BED JESUS ✤

In 1995, Shelly Penn purchased a bunk bed for her son, Joshua, at an auction. It wasn't until 2009, however, that she and her husband, John, discovered an image of Christ on the bed frame. "My late husband, William, died in 2000, and the family sees this as a message that he is watching over us," says Shelly, who is now remarried. "We feel blessed to have been chosen to receive this gift."

—DISCOVERED BY JOHN AND SHELLY PENN, MONCLOVA, OHIO

✤ BEDROOM DOOR JESUS ✤

Richard Morrison awoke one morning in 2006 to see a previously unnoticed image of Jesus on his bedroom door. When his wife awoke, she, too, saw it at once. "The door is still in our bedroom, keeping us safe and healthy," says Morrison.

—DISCOVERED BY RICHARD MORRISON, SAN DIEGO, CALIFORNIA

❧ LAVA LAMP MARY ☙

When John Smith first discovered this image of the Virgin Mary and baby Jesus in his lava lamp, he knew it was a blessing. "This is a true, tangible miracle that is not just an optical illusion," Smith says. "It is visible in all directions and permanently frozen in this shape." Smith has set up a shrine to the lava lamp in his home.

—REVEALED TO JOHN SMITH, SYDNEY, AUSTRALIA

❧ CHICKEN BREAST JESUS ❧

"In December of 2008, I ordered a grilled chicken breast and vegetables in an Italian restaurant," David Martin recalls. "After having eaten about half of the chicken, I brushed back the greens on the top, looked down, and saw the image. I told some colleagues at the table, 'I think Jesus is on my chicken.'" The chicken breast has been in a Ziploc bag at the bottom of Martin's refrigerator ever since.

—REVEALED TO DAVID MARTIN, SYRACUSE, NEW YORK

✥ CRYSTAL MARY ✥

In October of 2002, Rose Joyson and her sister, Ellen, went on a nature walk in the woods near her house. Ellen had been recently diagnosed with cancer, and these walks helped to soothe her. While searching for rocks along the riverbed, Rose spotted this crystal. "I knew deep down that it had come to me for a reason," she says. "I felt it was to give me the strength to be by my sister's side when she needed me the most, and to let her know it was all going to be all right."

—DISCOVERED BY ROSE JOYSON,
SHEPARTON, VICTORIA, AUSTRALIA

❦ KNOT SWIRL MARY ❦

In 2005, C. Ferguson discovered this image of the Virgin Mary in the knot swirls of a wooden fence on her property. An amateur photographer, she snapped a photo of the apparition and sent it off to be developed. "I couldn't believe my eyes when I first noticed it," Ferguson says, "but when I got the film developed, it was so very clear. I'm not a highly religious person, but when I pass our gate, I put my hand on the image to ask for strength. I feel a sense of peace come over me."

—DISCOVERED BY C. FERGUSON, PORTLAND, OREGON

✤ MEMORY FLASH CARD JESUS ✤

This image of Jesus, complete with beard and halo, manifested itself in a four-gig Samsung Flash memory chip at Chipworks in Castro Valley, California. Dick James, the company's spokesman, states, "We often get dark fringe lines in the silicon, and in this case it looks like there was some holy influence."

—SHARED BY DICK JAMES, CASTRO VALLEY, CALIFORNIA

❧ GREASE STAIN JESUS ❧

For years, Deb Serio had to side step a dripping can of driveway sealant whenever she walked through her garage. "My husband, John, insisted on keeping it for touch-ups, so it remained in the garage along with all of his other junk," she recalls. "But one day I just got fed up and threw it away." When she lifted the leaking can to toss it out, she noticed that it had left a grimy stain on the garage floor that bore the likeness of Christ.

—DISCOVERED BY DEB SERIO, FOREST, VIRGINIA

❧ CLOSET DOOR JESUS ❧

Wendy Divock was resting in her bedroom, eyes closed, when she felt a very light touch on her face. She opened her eyes expecting to see her husband, Jerry, but found that the room was empty. Instead, her eyes locked on an image of Jesus on her closet door that she hadn't noticed before. "It was not there until that day, and we have no idea how it got there," Divock says.

—REVEALED TO WENDY AND JERRY DIVOCK,
EAST WINDSOR, NEW JERSEY

❧ TREE ROOT JOSEPH ❧

Ingrid Towles was walking through her backyard when she saw a curious-looking root underneath one of her Cyprus palms. On closer inspection there appeared to be an image of Joseph holding the baby Jesus. Her friend Randy Moss cut the root from the rest of the tree, and it is now enshrined in a glass case in Towles's home.

**—UNEARTHED BY RANDY MOSS AND INGRID TOWLES,
PUNTA GORDA, FLORIDA**

❖ SHEET METAL JESUS ❖

In February of 2008, employee Thomas Haley was unloading supplies at Hardy's True Value Hardware when he spotted the face of Jesus Christ on a piece of sheet metal in Manchester, Connecticut. "I mean, it hasn't done anything miraculous yet, but seeing it is kind of groovy," says Haley. "It brightens people's day." Haley showed the sheet to his coworkers and customers, many of whom also recognized Jesus. Though some claimed that it looked more like rock legend Jim Morrison.

—REVEALED TO THOMAS HALEY, MANCHESTER, CONNECTICUT

❀ BUDDHA BEEHIVE ❀

In November of 2008, members of the Cambodian Buddhist
community in Rochester, Minnesota, discovered a beehive shaped
like a seated Buddha nestled in the eaves of their temple. "The
Buddha is trying to tell everybody to seek peace in their lives,"
says Voeun Sor, a community elder. Buddhist monk Sokunthea
Thun agrees: "Bees can do this kind of miracle, so humans can
also do miracles. Everywhere in this world, we humans need to
follow in the bees' path to make peace and serenity."

—APPEARED TO MEMBERS OF
THE CAMBODIAN BUDDHIST COMMUNITY,
ROCHESTER, MINNESOTA

✤ CHOCOLATE EASTER EGG JESUS ✤

On Easter in 2009, Eric Peterson's father and stepmom sent him a See's Candy chocolate and peanut butter egg. After pulling the decorative sugar flower off the top of the candy, Peterson noticed an image of Jesus's face in a chunk of chocolate stuck to the bottom of the flower. "I don't consider myself a religious person, and don't belong to a church, but I have to admit, finding an image of Jesus on Easter was a great experience, and I'm sure it will become a tradition to talk about it on Easters to come," Peterson says.

—APPEARED TO ERIC PETERSON, ROSEVILLE, CALIFORNIA

❧ TABLETOP MARY ❧

"My eighty-three-year-old mother volunteers at one of the historic Spanish Missions in California, and she asked me to carve something for their annual fiesta," recalls artist Bud Guzman. "I decided to make a tabletop on a flat piece of wood I bought at Home Depot." After finishing the piece he got "the proverbial chill" when he noticed the image of the Virgin Mary upon the table. "I truly don't know what to make of it," he says.

—REVEALED TO BUD GUZMAN, COALINGA, CALIFORNIA

✿ DOOR MOLDING JESUS ✿

In April of 2008, Tim Bunn discovered this image of Jesus on the door molding in the bathroom of his retail store, Pro-Mow Equipment Sales, in Raleigh, North Carolina. The image is visible in the lower area of the molding just to the left of the door. He pointed it out to a few of his employees and friends. "Almost everyone that looks at this image can see the face of Jesus, but some people also see other faces in the same damaged area of the door molding," Bunn explains.

—DISCOVERED BY TIM BUNN, GARNER, NORTH CAROLINA

❧ JESUS AND MARY STONE ❧

Upon examining this stone at an estate sale, Anthony Ditizio noticed that it contained an image of the Virgin Mary cradling baby Jesus, with a woman kneeling before them. When he turned it over, he was equally surprised to find another image on the other side—this one of the Virgin Mary staring up into the heavens with Jesus sitting on her lap. "Being a religious man, I bought it," he says. "I am not claiming the stone has any miraculous powers, but I thought it was wonderful."

—APPEARED TO ANTHONY DITIZIO, FT. LEE, NEW JERSEY

✥ COUCH STAIN JESUS ✥

After doing some spring cleaning in 2009, Kelly M. noticed a lingering stain on his couch. Hoping to eradicate it for good, he aggressively cleaned and scrubbed the spot again. Inspecting his work the next day, Kelly saw that his scrubbing had yielded an image of Jesus in what was left of the stain. "My wife and I aren't quite sure what the message is," he says, "although we are fairly recent converts to Christianity, so the image serves to reinforce what we have already begun to learn."

—APPEARED TO KELLY AND STEFANIE M.,
RAVENSDALE, WASHINGTON

❦ CELL PHONE JESUS ❧

Linda Square was scrolling though some family photos she had taken on her cell phone when she noticed a lone "dark and blurry" image among the pictures of smiling family members. When she turned the phone sideways, she recognized a shadowy image of Jesus, bearded and wearing a white robe, shrouded in white light. "My guess is that the phone was in a pocket or bag and somehow got triggered to become a camera," Square speculates.

—APPEARED TO LINDA SQUARE, PENSACOLA, FLORIDA

❧ VIRGIN MARY AND CHILD IN WOOD ❧

Laura Hazel discovered this piece of wood while she was walking through the woods in Patapsco State Park in Ellicott City, Maryland, in 2008. She studied it closely and saw the unmistakable figure of the Virgin Mary with a clearly defined neck and head holding the smaller figure of a baby. "Mary appears to have a halo and the baby Jesus has eyes where the wood has naturally started to soften," Hazel states. "There is a knot of wood where the baby's heart would be."

DISCOVERED BY LAURA HAZEL, ELLICOTT CITY, MARYLAND

❧ PAPER TOWEL JESUS ❧

Andrew Miller was at work when he noticed that the office's automated packaging system needed cleaning. "It's a machine that prints labels on boxes," he says, "and the print cartridge used to print those labels needed to be cleaned, so I wiped the print heads with a damp paper towel. A few hours later, while I was cleaning up the area I noticed the image of Jesus on the paper towel."

—SHARED BY ANDREW MILLER AND STEPHEN G. HESLER,
SYRACUSE, NEW YORK

❈ ALABASTER VASE JESUS ❈

Walter Chrysler was initially attracted to this alabaster vase because its colors matched the décor of his living room. However, it was when he noticed that it bore the likeness of Jesus that he had to have it. "Our friends think it's awesome that such a clear image of His face has naturally formed on this stone," Chrysler explains. "It's a topic of conversation whenever we have people over to our home."

—DISCOVERED BY WALTER CHRYSLER, PATASKALA, OHIO

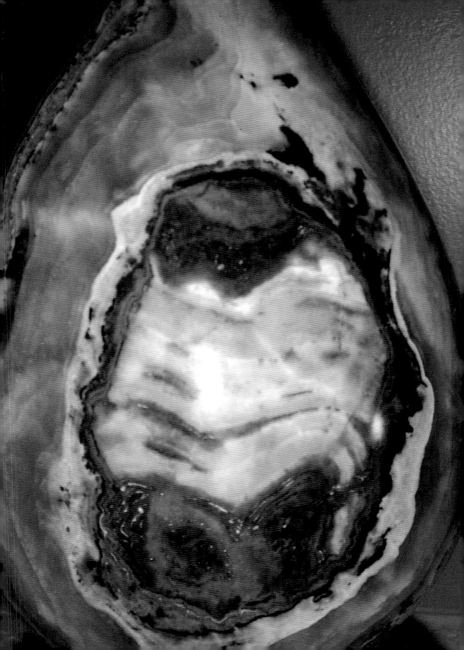

HARRY AND SANDRA CHORON are the authors of several books on popular culture. They live in Haworth, New Jersey.

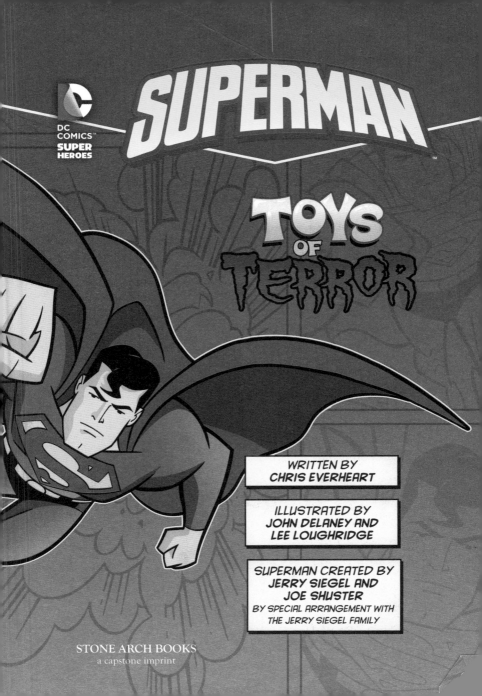

Published by Stone Arch Books
A Capstone Imprint
1710 Roe Crest Drive
North Mankato, Minnesota 56003
www.capstonepub.com

STAR13233

Library of Congress Cataloging-in-Publication Data
Everheart, Chris.
    The Toys of Terror / by Chris Everheart; illustrated by John Delaney.
    p. cm. — (DC Super Heroes. Superman)
    ISBN 978-1-4342-1156-9 (library binding)
    ISBN 978-1-4342-1374-7 (pbk.)
    ISBN 978-1-4342-6592-0 (ebook)
    [1. Superheroes—Fiction.] I. Delaney, John, ill. II. Title.
PZ7.7.E94Toy 2009
[Fic]—dc22   2008032428

Summary: Christmas dreams become nightmares when toys turn deadly. Only
one person can be behind all the mayhem — the Toyman!

Art Director: Bob Lentz
Designer: Bob Lentz

TABLE OF CONTENTS

CHAPTER 1

SURPRISE PACKAGES

The Christmas float pulled to a stop outside a toy store in downtown Metropolis. A crowd of little kids cheered. Reporters Clark Kent and Lois Lane made their way through the smiling faces. They were here to write a story for their newspaper, the *Daily Planet*.

"This is the biggest crowd I've ever seen for the Christmas parade," said Lois.

"The ad on TV said there would be free toys," Clark said. "That always attracts a crowd."

The two reporters stopped near the float. A huge Christmas tree stood in the middle of the float. It sparkled with colorful twinkling lights. A pile of brightly wrapped presents sat under it.

The children cheered, looking for the jolly old man with a white beard. Instead a big, beefy man stepped onto the float. He wore a red Santa suit. His boots and belt were as black as his hair. He had mean eyes and a scar on his right cheek.

The crowd went silent. Some of the children frowned. A few of them turned away.

"Clark, isn't that —?" Lois began to ask.

Clark gave a quick nod. "Bruno 'Ugly' Mannheim," he said.

"Wasn't he in jail?" Lois asked.

"He was in jail," said Clark. "Superman caught him robbing a bank last year."

"Then what's he doing on that float?" asked Lois.

Clark watched Bruno closely. "Maybe he's here to steal Christmas," he joked.

Just then Bruno Mannheim spoke up. "Hello, children," he said. "I am so happy to see all of you! You see, I just got out of jail. I learned a lot while paying for my crimes. I have been a bad, bad man. But starting today, I'm going to change." Bruno looked over at Clark and Lois.

"So that's his game," said Clark. "He wants us to think he's a good guy now."

Bruno raised his hands and continued, "Children of Metropolis, these are my gifts to you!"

Bruno reached under the tree and grabbed an armful of presents. He started throwing colorful boxes into the crowd. The children cheered.

"The kids certainly think he's a good guy now!" said Lois.

As the parade float neared the reporters, Bruno looked down at Lois. "Miss Lane, would you join me on the float?" he asked politely, holding out his hand. "You've been my toughest critic. I want to show you exactly how much I've changed."

Lois smiled and took a step toward the float. Clark Kent quickly grabbed her arm. "Be careful, Lois," he warned. "I have a funny feeling about this."

Lois smiled. "What's the matter?" she asked. "Jealous that I'm getting the scoop?"

Lois grabbed Bruno's hand and stepped onto the float. Wrapping paper was flying everywhere. The children shouted with joy as they saw their presents.

"You see, Miss Lane?" Bruno said, looking out at the crowd. "I've learned my lesson. I'm all about spreading joy and happiness."

Lois pointed toward the back of the float. A group of tough-looking men stood on the street, frowning. "If you're such a good guy, Bruno, why are those thugs still hanging around? They don't look joyful or happy to me," she said.

"Them?" said Bruno, smiling. "They're my bodyguards."

"You can fool children with a few gifts," said Lois. "But you can't fool me."

Bruno's mouth turned up in a crooked grin. "That hurts, Miss Lane," he said. Then he waved to some kids in the crowd. "Come up on the float, kids! Show everyone your presents."

Five kids jumped on the float. One boy waved his box. "It's a helicopter!" he shouted. "Cool!"

Bruno scowled. "A helicopter?" he asked, slightly puzzled.

A little girl held an open box over her head. "I got a helicopter, too!" she exclaimed.

All of the children opened boxes to discover the same toy.

"Those were supposed to be dolls and toy soldiers!" Bruno muttered. "What's going on?"

Suddenly, a girl screamed. Her little helicopter zoomed out of its box and flew around her head. Then all the other boxes burst apart. Every helicopter started flying.

WHIR-WHIR-WHIR-WHIR!!

The choppers circled the crowd. They buzzed just above the kids' heads. The tiny cannons on the toys squirted a sticky, yellow-orange liquid. The children screamed and started to run.

CHAPTER 2

RUNAWAY FLOAT

The little helicopters swarmed toward the float. Lois ducked the whirling blades.

"So this was your plan, Bruno?" she shouted. "This is bad even for you!"

Bruno waved off an attacking helicopter. "This wasn't supposed to happen!" he said. "I stole a load of dolls and toy soldiers from a warehouse! Someone switched them for these nasty choppers!"

Clark Kent called from the street, "Lois, look out!"

A group of helicopters circled in the air above the kids and their parents. Any second now, it looked like they were going to shoot more sticky liquid from their guns.

Near the float, Bruno's men were also dodging the helicopters. One crook pulled out a huge pistol and started shooting into the air, aiming to hit a helicopter.

BANG! He missed. The choppers attacked the thugs like a flock of angry metal birds. The men yelled and jumped into a nearby car for safety.

Clark looked around to make sure no one was watching him. Then he inhaled and blew out a huge super-breath. The circling helicopters went spinning away on the wind. Clark kept blowing until the dangerous toys were blown far down the street.

"The helicopters are flying away!" a kid yelled.

"Let's get out of here!" shouted another.

Then Clark heard tires screeching. He looked over to see Bruno's Christmas float jump forward and speed away. Clark knew this was serious trouble. He started looking for a place to slip away and change into his Superman uniform.

The car carrying Bruno's thugs tore off after the float. They didn't want to let their boss get away without them.

On the float, Lois and the kids screamed. Bruno grabbed hold of the Christmas tree. He fell backward, tearing off a branch. Presents flew off the float and scattered into the street.

"Who's driving the float?" yelled Lois.

"I don't know," Bruno answered.

Lois tried to gather the kids. "Lay down flat," she told them. "Hold on tight!"

Bruno was frightened. He shouted below to where the driver sat, "Stop this thing! Now!"

"You won't get away with kidnapping me and these children, Bruno!" shouted Lois.

"I'm not doing this!" Bruno cried.

The float raced down the street. It took a sharp turn around a corner.

Lois was thrown sideways and rolled across the deck of the float. To her surprise, she found herself staring into a small window in front of the driver.

Even though Lois was bundled up against the cold, a deep shiver went down her back. She realized now that Bruno Mannheim was telling the truth. The out-of-control float was not his idea. Lois could see into the driver's seat. She saw an evil smile, staring eyes, and a little bow tie. The crazy driver was not one of Bruno's men. It was Bruno's enemy.

The Toyman!

CHAPTER 3

THE TOYMAN

The Toyman always wore a mask with a horrible grin, but at this moment he sounded angry. "Move aside, Miss Lane!" he shouted. "I can't see where I'm going! Do you want me to have an accident?"

"Toyman!" shouted Lois. "I should have known!"

"But you didn't," the Toyman snapped. "My plan was perfect. And it's working."

"Attacking children with helicopters?" Lois said. "You should be ashamed!"

The float swerved as the Toyman jerked the wheel to the right. Lois held on tight.

"Bruno's the one who should be ashamed," the Toyman shouted. "He thinks he can clean up his image by giving away a few toys? Hah! I'll show him!"

Bruno crawled over to the window beside Lois Lane. His face was red with anger. "Toyman, you'll be sorry for this," he said.

The Toyman laughed. "You're the one who's going to be sorry," he said. "You'll wish that you'd never killed my father!"

"I didn't kill your father," Bruno said. "He killed himself!"

"Because you ruined his business!" shouted Toyman. "Now you'll finally pay!" He turned the steering wheel sharply. Bruno and Lois rolled away from the window.

The Toyman looked in his rearview mirror. He saw the black car filled with Bruno's men. They were close behind and catching up to the float.

"Here are some toys for your boys to play with," the Toyman sneered.

He pulled a lever next to the seat. A hatch opened under the float's rear bumper. Ten little windup robots dropped onto the street. They wandered around in circles, cranking and buzzing. When the black car reached them, the robots started exploding.

In the car, one of the thugs yelled, "Look out!" The driver swerved around the bursting robots. But the explosion rocked the car. The windows were blown out.

"Bruno must be crazy!" one of the men shouted. "Why is he trying to stop us?"

Toyman looked at the street ahead. There, standing in the middle of the road was a tall figure in red and blue. Superman!

"Drat his super-speed!" Toyman said to himself. "Those helicopters should have kept him busy longer."

Superman watched the float race toward him and the black car follow behind. Using his X-ray vision, Superman searched the inside of the float. There, in the driver seat, he recognized the Toyman. The children and Lois were in serious danger!

The Toyman pushed a button on the dashboard. "Good thing I planned for this," he said.

Superman saw a small door open on the front of the float. "What's he up to now?" Superman wondered.

A blast shot out of the little door like a machine gun. Superman saw a flock of yellow rubber duckies coming at him. They looked so cute and harmless. But Superman knew Toyman better. He wasn't surprised when the first ducky began to swell up like a giant balloon.

QUACKKKKK!

All of the duckies began to grow larger. Their rubbery sides stuck together. Soon, they had turned into a huge yellow barrier surrounding the Man of Steel. Then they puffed up even more. Superman was trapped inside a gigantic ball of rubber.

"Nice try, Toyman," said Superman.

The hero began to spin. The yellow ducky balloons spun around with him. Faster and faster he whirled. The yellow rubber moved so quickly that it began to burn up. Soon, it had sizzled away. Bits of burning rubber duckies littered the street.

"Superman! Help!" cried Lois from the speeding float.

The kids' eyes were wide with fear. "Superman!" they screamed.

Superman decided he could catch up to the float in a minute. First he would take care of Bruno's thugs. He jumped back into the road. He set his feet down on the street and reached forward. The black car sped toward him. When the men inside saw the super hero, they all shouted at once. The tires skidded and screeched, but it was too late.

The car slammed right into the Man of Steel. The front end folded up as if it hit a telephone pole. Superman skidded backward as the car ground to a stop. The radiator smoked. The engine coughed and sputtered.

The thugs looked up at Superman, shocked and amazed.

"Sorry boys," Superman said. "I can't risk you running into someone while I'm trying to save your boss. I'll take care of Bruno and the Toyman."

"Toyman?" muttered one of the crooks. "Is he behind all this?"

Superman shot up into the air and out of sight.

CHAPTER 4

THE TOY FACTORY OF TERROR

The Toyman chuckled when he knew Superman was no longer in sight. He drove the float into a tunnel and descended below the city streets. The kids were scared in the dark. They huddled close to Lois.

"Where are we going?" Lois shouted.

"Yeah," said Bruno, "where do you think you're taking us?"

The Toyman didn't answer. Instead, he stopped the float in the middle of the tunnel. Steel doors opened in front of them.

Meanwhile, in the sky above Metropolis, Superman flew in search of the Toyman's float. He used his super-vision to magnify the streets below. He followed the route where Toyman and the float should have gone. But they were missing. Where could they be?

Underground, the float rolled through the steel doors. Inside was an old factory, piled high with broken toy parts. Dolls' heads and toy soldiers' arms were heaped on the floor. A thousand jack-in-the-boxes without the jacks leaned against the walls.

When the float finally stopped, Lois, Bruno, and the children got off. The strange scene scared the kids more than the dark tunnel. Some began to cry.

"Don't worry," said Lois. "Superman will find us. This will all be over soon."

The Toyman emerged from the float and looked down at his prisoners. His eyes were cruel and cold above his wide smile. "Yes. Don't worry, kids. Bruno will be finished soon," he told them.

"Let the kids go, Toyman," said Lois. "They didn't do anything to you."

"I don't care about them," the Toyman said. "I'm after Bruno. He owes me. He owes me big. And nothing will stop me."

Bruno Mannheim stood up. "Take the kids, Toyman," he said. "You can ransom them back to their parents. You'll make a fortune. Just let me go."

Lois turned to the crook who was still dressed in his Santa outfit. "Why, you rat!" she said. "These are innocent kids. Be a man and face the Toyman yourself!"

Bruno waved a hand. "Ah, Toyman won't hurt them. Especially since they're worth so much money."

CLINK CLINK CLINK

Lois turned to see the Toyman walking up a set of steel stairs. The mask with its weird grin was still stuck on his face.

"Too bad these kids trusted Bruno," the Toyman said. "If they're foolish enough to trust this crook, they deserve what they get."

Soon the Toyman had reached a platform high above the factory floor. He pulled a remote control out of this sweater pocket. "I've built a special toy for you, Bruno," he said. "I think your new young friends will enjoy it." Toyman pushed a button on the remote control.

Lois heard a bounce and a squeak. The noise grew louder. The kids pushed themselves closer. She hugged them tightly. **BOUNCE! SQUEAK!** A soccer ball bounced out from behind a pile of toy cars. It stopped in the middle of the floor.

Everyone relaxed. Lois sighed, and Bruno smiled.

"What's that supposed to be?" Bruno laughed. "You're going to kill me with a soccer ball?"

"It's so much more than a soccer ball," said the Toyman from his perch. He pushed another button on the remote. "Let's play," he said.

ZZRRRRTT! ZZRRRRTT! The soccer ball started to vibrate. Everyone closed their eyes, expecting it to blow up.

But instead of exploding, it opened with a **SNAP!** A dozen blades, sharp as razors, poked out of the ball. The ball started rolling across the floor. The squeak was gone. The sharp blades scraped as they moved against the concrete.

The children screamed.

The soccer ball rolled toward them. Lois grabbed the kids. She pulled them away from the deadly ball.

"Toyman, don't do this!" shouted Lois. She looked up at his perch. The little villain's evil mask glowed with happiness.

"I've finally got Bruno Mannheim right where I want him," the Toyman said. "I have him trapped, and Superman can't get in my way. It's brilliant. Don't you think, Miss Lane?"

Lois was scared. "Turn Bruno over to the police," she pleaded. "Let them take care of him."

"My super soccer ball is much more efficient, Miss Lane," Toyman said. He jumped back onto the floor and laughed. "And when it's done, there won't be anything left to find."

Lois looked over and saw Bruno climbing the Christmas tree on the float. "Get back here, you coward!" she shouted.

Bruno looked down at her and the kids. "Forget it, lady. You're on your own," he called.

The soccer ball turned toward Lois and the children. It chased them into a corner. The knives were flashing and slicing through the air.

CHAPTER 5

TRAPPED!

"My life's work is almost done," the Toyman said. "I'll finally avenge my father's death."

"But these kids have fathers, too," said Lois, still huddling close to the children on the floor.

"Boo hoo," said the Toyman with a laugh.

"Hurry, children," shouted Lois. She pulled them back onto the float. "I think we'll be safe up here."

"Oh no!" shouted one of the kids.

A thin metal arm reached out of the soccer ball. It grabbed the side of the float and pulled itself up. The soccer ball started climbing onto the float. It was only three feet away from the kids. They started to back away but couldn't go any further.

"Quick," said Lois. "Jump!"

The children jumped to the floor. Just then, the blades on the ball spun like circular saws. They cut a path through the float like a soft stick of butter.

All eyes turned to the ceiling. A ray of sunlight poured through a hole. Then suddenly, the children saw a different ray of hope.

"Superman!" the children shouted.

In a second, Superman was on the float.
He kicked the soccer ball away. The toy and
its blades bounced against the factory wall.

"Blast you, Superman!" shouted the
Toyman.

The Toyman pushed another button on his remote control. At his command, the soccer ball bounced off the wall and came flying back. This time it was spinning a hundred times faster than before.

"You won't ruin my revenge, Superman!" shouted the Toyman. "I'll cut you to super ribbons!"

Lois pointed and shouted, "Superman, look out!"

Superman turned and saw the soccer ball. It cut through the air at lightning speed. Superman spun on one foot and threw a back kick. The ball bounced off his heel and flew toward the Toyman.

The little villain punched frantically at more buttons on his remote control. It was too late.

The bladed soccer ball spun upward and then crashed down in front of him. Sparks flew off the metal. Then the ball flew past the Toyman, shredding his bow tie.

"Aaaahhhhhh!" Toyman screamed.

The ball smashed into the ceiling above his head and smashed into pieces.

The Toyman ducked, trying to avoid the falling metal blades. His tiny shoe slipped on the floor. He fell backward and landed in a pile of empty jack-in-the-boxes.

"No!" he cried.

Hundreds of boxes tumbled down, trapping the Toyman beneath their combined weight.

As the boxes moved, their handles turned. The factory was filled with the happy sounds of "Pop Goes the Weasel."

"I don't think this little weasel is going to pop up anytime soon," said Superman.

He turned to Lois and the children. "Don't worry, kids," he said. "You'll be back with your parents soon."

"Are you all right, Miss Lane?" Superman asked.

Just then, Bruno Mannheim climbed down from the top of the Christmas tree. "Whoa, that was close," he said. "What took you so long?"

Superman grinned. Then he looked at the dark factory. "The walls of Toyman's hideout are made of lead. I wasn't able to use my X-ray vision to find you.

"That slowed me down a little," Superman continued. "But then, thanks to Miss Lane's clues, I soon followed you here."

Bruno and the kids stared at her. "Her clues?" asked the crook.

"Yes," said Superman. "Miss Lane dropped her shoes along the road. Then she dropped her notepad. I followed the direction of the clues, and it led me straight to this abandoned building."

Lois looked down at her bare feet. Her shoes must have fallen off when the Toyman swerved the float back and forth along the road. In all the excitement, she hadn't even noticed they were gone.

"Quick thinking, Miss Lane," said Superman.

"Uh, thanks," she said.

Bruno held his hand out to the super hero. "Well, thanks loads, Superman," he said. "It's nice to be working together for a change. See you later."

"I've got someone coming to pick you up, Bruno," said Superman.

Bruno smiled. "My boys?" he asked, hopefully.

"No, *my* boys," Superman smiled.

A police siren sounded in the distance.

"Hey, wait a minute!" shouted Bruno. "The Toyman was after me. He was trying to kill me. I'm the victim here."

"And what about all those stolen presents you were going to hand out at the parade?" asked Superman.

Bruno frowned. "Oh, right." He looked at the broken dolls and soldiers that littered the Toyman's factory. The little villain had replaced them with his helicopters in the warehouse that Bruno had broken into earlier.

Lois stepped up to Superman. "I don't know how to thank you, Superman," she said. "You're always nearby when I —" She noticed the kids staring up at the Man of Steel. "I mean, when we need you."

"I wish I could stay, Miss Lane," he said, "but there's more crime to fight in Metropolis. The holidays are always a busy time."

"I can't wait to get back to the *Daily Planet* and write this story," said Lois. "Poor Clark is missing out on the whole thing."

Superman smiled. "Oh, I get the feeling Clark is nearby," he said.

The Man of Steel waved at the kids. He then grabbed Toyman and shot up through the hole in the roof. He became a red and blue streak, then disappeared.

"Well, kids," said Lois, staring up at the empty sky. "Merry Christmas."

DAILY PLANET

FROM THE DESK OF CLARK KENT

WHO IS THE TOYMAN?

Winslow Schott Jr. watched his father create wondrous toys for children. He hoped to one day follow in his father's footsteps. However, Winslow's dreams were shattered when his father was framed by gangster Bruno Mannheim and sent to prison. The experience twisted little Winslow's creative mind, transforming him into the Toyman. Armed with an arsenal of deadly toys, the Toyman pursues Bruno Mannheim, terrorizing all of Metropolis in the process.

- Bruno Mannheim agreed to finance Schott Sr.'s toy factory, but used the facility as a front for his dirty dealings. When the Gotham Police descended upon the factory, Schott took the fall, leaving little Winslow to grow up in orphanages.

- Schott Jr. has been know to toy with his foes. Once, Superman thought he had finally captured Schott, but the real Toyman flipped a switch and detonated a radio-controlled double!

- The Toyman isn't concerned with the safety of children. He often devises schemes that take advantage of them. In an attempt to frame the Man of Steel, the Toyman once designed Superman dolls that turned on their owners.

- Unable to relate with others, Schott once created a living doll to give himself a friend. Named Darci Mason, the living doll resembled a real human in every way. Later, Darci left the Toyman to become a famous fashion model.

BIOGRAPHIES

Chris Everheart always dreamed of interesting places, fascinating people, and exciting adventures. He is still a dreamer. He enjoys writing thrilling stories about young heroes who live in a world that doesn't always understand them. Chris lives in Minneapolis, Minnesota, with his family. He plans to travel to every continent on the globe, see interesting places, meet fascinating people, and have exciting adventures.

John Delaney is an award-winning storyboard artist, director, animator and design artist with over 20 years of experience in both live-action production and animation. For the past 15 years John has also worked as a comic book artist for DC Comics and Bongo Comics. He has pencilled a wide variety of characters such as Superman, Batman, Wonder Woman, and the Justice League, as well as shows like *Dexter's Laboratory*, *Scooby-Doo*, *Futurama*, *The Simpsons*, and many more.

Lee Loughridge has been working in comics for more than 14 years. He currently resides in sunny California in a tent on the beach.

GLOSSARY

avenge (uh-VENJ)—pay someone back for wrongdoings

coward (KOW-ard)—someone who is easily scared and runs away from scary situations

descended (di-SEND-id)—went downward

inhaled (in-HAYLD)—breathed in

frantically (FRAN-tik-uhl-ee)—did something wildly with excitement or fear

lever (LEV-ur)—a bar that you use to control a machine

ransom (RAN-suhm)—money that is demanded before a prisoner will be set free

scattered (SKAT-urd)—moved hurriedly in different directions

scoop (SKOOP)—a story reported in a newspaper before others have a chance to report it

villain (VIL-uhn)—a wicked or evil person

DISCUSSION QUESTIONS

1. Bruno tries to give children toys to make everybody like him. Do you think his desire to change from bad to good was real? Why or why not?

2. Superman gives Lois credit for something she did on accident. Have you ever been thanked, or punished, for something you didn't mean to do? Explain.

3. Do you think Superman should keep his true identity secret? What would be the positives and negatives of telling everyone that he is Clark Kent?

WRITING PROMPTS

1. Superman's secret identity is Clark Kent, mild-mannered reporter. If you had a secret identity, what would it be? How would living two lives be challenging?

2. The Toyman has created lots weird toys. Create a plan for your own toy. What does it look like? What does it do? After you explain how it works, draw a picture of your new toy.

3. The people of Metropolis hold a parade as a celebration of the holidays. What celebrations do you participate in? Which celebration was your favorite? Why?